# CONTENTS

**1** FROM THE DESK OF THE PRESIDENT

**6** REGGIE WALKER

**11** DAVID CARTER

**15** CYNTHIA DAVIS

**22** MITCH RUSSO

**27** MICHAEL MARKIEWICZ

**33** HERB LANG

**38** CHASE BARFIELD

On the cover: Reggie Walker and David Carter. See their stories on pages 6 and 11.

## PIVOT Magazine

**Founder and President**
Jason Miller
jason@strategicadvisorboard.com

**Editor-in-Chief**
Chris O'Byrne
chris@jetlaunch.net

**Design**
JETLAUNCH.net

**Advertising**
Chris O'Byrne
chris@jetlaunch.net

**Webmaster**
Joel Phillips
joel@proshark.com

**Editor**
Laura West
laura@jetlaunch.net

**Cover Design**
Debbie O'Byrne

## FROM THE EDITOR

The next two issues are special editions to highlight a few of the incredible members who are part of The Bellwether Alliance.

Since being introduced to The Bellwether Alliance and subsequently interviewing several members (including the Viceroy), I've been deeply impressed by the level of character and servant leadership displayed.

Instead of giving each article in this magazine a title, we chose to simply use the name of the Bellwether member highlighted.

As you'll see as you read through the articles, the breadth of experience of Bellwether members is vast. Yet, each one follows the principles and credo and strives to grow and serve.

You can learn more about The Bellwether Alliance at thebellwetheralliance.com.

# FROM THE DESK OF THE PRESIDENT

## Leading The Old-Fashioned Way

**Melanie Fine, Contributor, *Forbes Magazine***

Between 1979 to 1986, Ogilvy & Mather cast actor John Houseman in 18 Smith Barney ads, voicing the now-famous line, "They make money the old-fashioned way, they earn it."

So what exactly is the old-fashioned way? Making your money work for you? Or, is it making your business acumen and superpower work for you, time and again?

I sat down with Jason Miller, founder of the Strategic Advisor Board (SAB), about what it takes to make a business successful and scalable. He should know. He has built and sold many successful companies over his career and is currently chair of 11 other companies in addition to SAB.

As an owner of multiple successful businesses, he joins the ranks of multi-business owners such as Elon Musk, who has owned many different businesses over the years, such as PayPal, Tesla Motors, and SpaceX, Richard Branson, whose Virgin Group controls more than 400 companies, and Warren Buffett, CEO of Berkshire Hathaway, whose website lists over 62 subsidiary companies, among them Duracell, See's Candy, and Geico.

Here's what Jason told me.

### 1. Be willing to do the hard work

"I grew up on a farm. Every morning at five o'clock I used to get up and my dad would give me a big scoop shovel and make me shovel around a ton of grain into all the feeders for the sheep," said Jason. "And I often would look over and see a farm hand right there, one scoop done. And I didn't understand. This doesn't make any sense when you're nine years old. But then later

got lucky. He says if you consider working seven days a week, 160 hours a week for 10 years before I really made it, luck. Okay. But no, it's about putting in the work.

Does hard work always translate over to money? No, but we shouldn't expect it to. What we should expect it to do is create relationships. The relationships create the money. Because the relationships do the good work."

## 2. The real work is in building relationships

"It takes a very long time of building a relationship with somebody. It takes hours and hours of conversations with Bob, let's say, about what he does, the things he does, and

on in life, looking back, I realize that was a valuable lesson in hard work and seeing it through. My dad's drive morphed into me, and that's what forces me every day to get up jazzed about everything that I do."

> " **People want to build million-dollar businesses overnight and never work a day in their lives. That's counter to the laws of nature.** "

People want to build million-dollar businesses overnight and never work a day in their lives. That's counter to the laws of nature that a farm exemplifies. There's plenty of hard work to be done. And nothing happens without the preparatory work, the care and feeding, and the sowing at the proper time and season.

"My wife always says," Miller continues, "that's one thing nobody can ever say about me is that I wasn't willing to do the work. Take Elon Musk for example. People say he

what his superpowers are. And it's not just a feeling, it's getting to know somebody.

"It's like being on the golf course and getting to know people and bringing back the way it used to be where people had conversations and they talked and it wasn't just a 15-minute call on Zoom. You don't get authenticity through a 15-minute call on Zoom. You have to do the work."

Miller's 11 companies are the result of building relationships and putting the right people in the right place.

"It's the result of a lot of hours talking to people," Miller continues. "But it's what I love to do. When you love to do something, it's not work.

"When somebody comes to me and says, here's what I think my problems are. And then I get in there and say, well, actually that wasn't a problem, but you got four stacked up over here that you've been ignoring. Then I can go to one of my family trees of business that I have, and I can plug those in and fix all those problems. And there are a couple of really good things about that. Number one, I know the guy that owns them. That's helpful. Two, I know the job will get done right. So I can back that 100%.

"And that's really what I set out to do was to create this all-encompassing solution for any business owner, young, new, or established, and be able to go in there and say, look, here are some of the issues that you have. Let me plug these things into it, to help you fix those problems. And it truly is a one-stop shop with which I can take any business leader and fix all their problems to help them grow and scale their companies."

## 3. Double down on your superpower

According to Miller, each of us has only two to three superpowers. The sooner we realize it, the better. Once you know your superpowers, delegate the rest. Miller's superpowers, in his own words, are hyper-growth/hyper-scale, strategic and operational implementation, and micro-pivots.

In forming the Strategic Advisor Board (SAB), he selected nine other people with superpowers complementary to, though different from, his. The combination of superpowers is the backbone and strength of SAB, much like the Avengers of the business world.

"For example, if you're very operational minded and you're trying to be the visionary for the company, that's probably not the right fit," explains Miller. "And that's okay if you own the company. Step down, take a chair role and put a CEO in place who is a visionary who can take the company where it needs to go.

## 4. Employ the military formula

"I joined the military at 17. I spent 23 years in the military, serving other people. And the military really gave me the formula, the leadership, those things that one really needs to understand operationally how to function in business—not by working in it,

> **Once you know your superpowers, delegate the rest.**

"Get out of your own and the company's way and work in your zone of genius. Perhaps you are more of a product person. Then you need to be in the hands-on development part. Be good at that. And then bring somebody else in to run the company itself. They're two very different roles for sure.

"When you can bring all the right players to the table, it just creates magic."

but in working on it, operationally speaking. And it really took me down the path to become a collector of businesses and be able to raise them and bring them to where I wanted them to be."

I asked Jason what formula the military taught him. Here's what he said.

"Well, it's complicated, because not everybody is the same. And when you ask most military leaders, why don't you treat Jim the same as you do Sally as you do Bob as you do Bill, they'll tell you it's because we're all different people. So when you look at this mix of different people, nothing is ever the same.

"The formula is fluid. It's getting to know people. People will tell you everything they need and what they're missing just that by having a conversation.

"While there is a specific formula that we take into a company, it's the people that influence all of that internally that doesn't make it cookie cutter. One company does it this way, whereas another does it that way. Not one of my companies operates the same because there are people involved."

"Every business, everybody has their challenges. So it's finding out how to best serve that client in the best way, based off of their talent, based off of their challenges and based off of their personality type."

"What I love the most," concludes Miller, "is being able to serve people and serve them as long as it takes, and give value for as long as it takes. And I think if we do that as leaders, as business owners, and as people, the world will be a better place. Because the truth is we live in a kind of an angry world right now, and kindness is free. It doesn't cost anything. So we can use all that we have as business people, as leaders, and as people, and use that as a vessel to do a lot of good."

First published in *Forbes* magazine at forbes.com/sites/melaniefine/2022/09/16/leading-the-old-fashioned-way

# REGGIE WALKER

I came from the hood, where there were hardly any mentors. I learned how to do things by seeing the bad examples and doing the exact opposite. There weren't a lot of examples of what to do to create the life that you want to live. While I only had a handful of mentors, I became a big recruit. While I was in college, I got introduced to the business and political sides of sports, and that was a big reason why, even though I came in with twenty-four people, only four of us finished.

It was the same thing with the NFL. You learn to understand the business side and the political side of things. That whole process chews up and spits a lot of kids out. That's the process that I felt was most important for people to understand when getting into this environment—understanding how it works and finding the best way to navigate through it.

It was important to me to help people transition out successfully because that was the other part of things that I realized throughout my career. When people get out of the NFL, they don't really go on to do anything. They're just stuck. I got really tired of seeing that.

What I considered success in that situation is that I was an undrafted free agent and worked my way up to a team captain. I made big plays and did what I wanted on the field. And then, I left on my own terms. I felt like that was a huge win.

But I felt that there were more people who could have had these wins and should have had these wins. I knew something needed to be done. In order to fix this problem, I felt like I had to take this all on myself because it's not something that you're going to understand how to convey to people who need to hear it if you haven't done it personally. And I knew that the people who needed to hear it were only going to hear it a certain way.

So, I started writing. Originally, it was just going to be a book. I started writing at 3:00 a.m. one morning. I saw a YouTube video that said that if you want to start something, you should just start right then and there. And I was just like, "You know what? You're right." So, I just started writing. I just did it. It got me at the exact right time, too.

I wrote the book, and then three years later, I wrote a course to accompany the book. The course goes into some of the teachings of the book. The course has gone through all these different changes. At first, it was just going to be a workbook, and then it was going to be a course. Then, we were going to do workshops. So now, we're trying to figure out the best way of presenting it. And then we'll figure out how to get it into the right heads.

It's been crazy and extremely difficult, nonetheless, because I created the course, but it is also college accredited. It took us years to complete that process. We had to decide the best way to sell it and figure out what people were actually looking for. We went through one of the hardest accreditation processes that a course can go through.

David Carter, my business partner, helped me co-create the course. When it came to this project in itself, I wrote it, but he was the one who got it to the place where it needed to be. He brought his connections, strategic help, and understanding of things, and he got me to look at it a lot bigger than I even looked at it. It's just been him and me every day, processing and creating together.

David and I hit it off the first day we met. I was in Arizona playing for the Cardinals before he got there. I had been playing for a year or two. His first day, he came in, I think we were doing physicals or just getting ourselves checked out, and we just looked at each other, and it was just like, "Hey man, what's up?" He was like, "What's up? How's it going?" And we've been talking since. It was very easy. It felt like we might have been brothers or something in another life. It was too easy, oddly easy. We've been great friends ever since. And it's amazing to continue to work together to do things that are important to us.

The course is for student-athletes to understand the processes that they're going through as they try to make it as athletes. It helps them understand relationships in this environment. It's essentially all about being a successful student-athlete before, during, and after their careers are over.

These kids are young. They are just becoming adults and get pressured into a situation where it's their job to be a full-time student and full-time athlete. A few months ago, they had 10:00 p.m. curfews, and suddenly, they're expected to be completely on their marks, on their squares with everything that they're doing with both their schoolwork and being an athlete, even though it is all new to them. They're a big person on campus now. Everyone knows who they are. As soon as they're freshmen, even if people don't know their name, they know that they're an athlete, and everywhere they go, they get attention. Everywhere.

When it comes to understanding the business and politics of things, now, they're a big revenue generator for the school, and they know it, the school knows it, everybody knows it. And they know that school athletics play a major role in getting people to the school. That pressure that's getting put on them, too, from trying to figure out how to navigate two full-time jobs, being young and still developing, and being famous now.

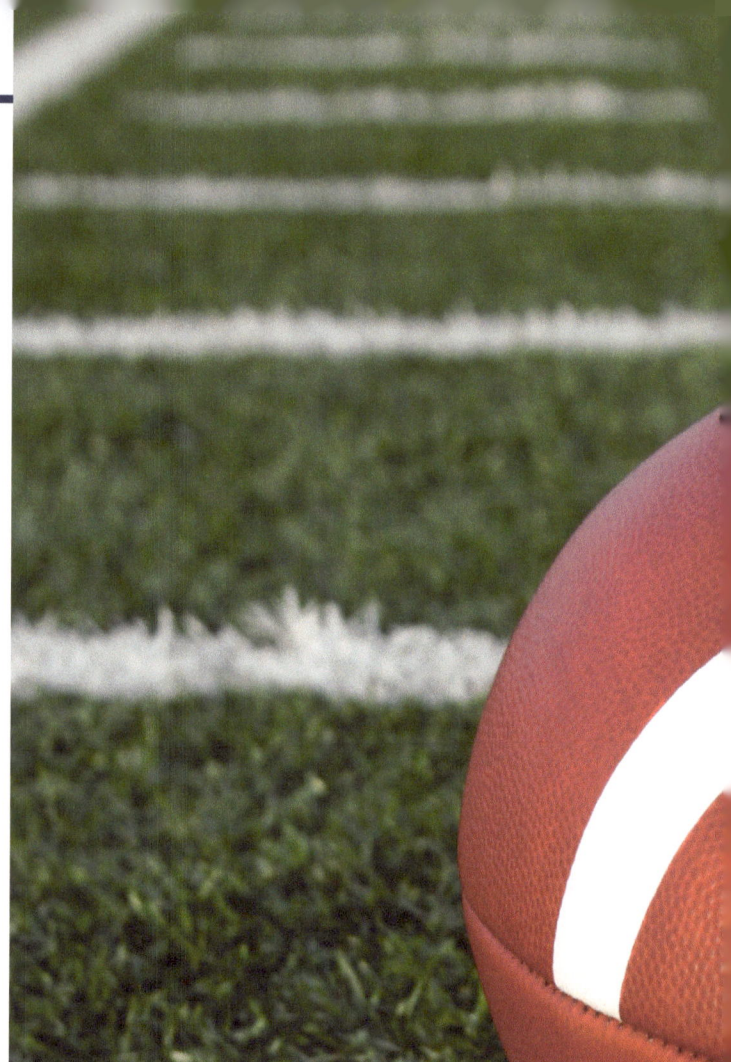

> Athletes must understand how to cultivate relationships with people because they want and need people fighting for them.

Even in their own little pocket, they're famous. They still have this goal of *I want to go professional. I want to go professional.* Some kids may want to be doctors or engineers, but most athletes want to go pro or be in the Olympics. They want to go to whatever the pinnacle of their sport is. That's how we're all driven.

And then, they have all these pitfalls like, *Man, I can make my own schedule. I can do what I want. I can party. I can drink. I can do*

*drugs. I can have all these wild escapades. I can do whatever I want now. My mom and dad aren't watching me anymore.*

And then you add in the political side of sports and teams. It's not about talent all the time. It's not about just being good at my sport. It's not about being the biggest, strongest, toughest, and fastest. That only plays a small part in sports. Athletes must understand how to cultivate relationships with people because they want and need people fighting for them behind closed doors. So, they really need to understand how to build relationships.

There are so many different elements to consider when going from college to professional, and I wanted to create this course so athletes could better understand everything involved. It's a one-stop shop. You're going to get all of it. You even learn about coaches and that they aren't your parents. You learn how to view them as your boss.

With some bosses, you can have that mother, father, or friend relationship. With some bosses, you can't. And at the end of the day, you're there to win. The whole point is winning. If they're not winning and you're not winning, you both are screwed. So, everything, when it comes to that relationship, has to be built around that

precedent. All this fun stuff is cool, but if we're losing, it doesn't matter.

I have kids to feed. I have goals and aspirations of my own as a coach. I have things that I want to accomplish in my life. And they must understand that as a college player, it's not the same relationship that they had with their high school coaches. Yeah, it was great, but this isn't high school anymore.

And then, it's the same thing when jumping from college to professional. It really is a business. Your coach is your boss. They'll tell you straight up, "I am your boss. I have bosses over me, but you better look at this at the end of the day because if I'm not winning, if we're not winning, I'm screwed, and you're screwed." It's the same in college too, but it's just not widely told to them point-blank. There are a lot of things that aren't explained well, and we provide that in this course.

I break it all down and help them understand their why because that's important for their drive going forward—during their playing careers and afterward. They need to figure that out first because understanding their why, their bigger vision, helps to put everything in place during their career and afterward. I don't want them to skip a beat once they're done.

Especially when it comes to football, which has a 100 percent injury rate. It's not *if* you'll get an injury but *when* you'll get one. Any play could be your last. All sports carry a risk of injury, and every injury could be your last. Therefore, having that bigger vision and knowing that is essential to keep as your base.

It is also important to know what your strengths and weaknesses are. This is especially true when you enter this environment where you must continuously get better and stronger. But you're not getting better and stronger if you're not being real about yourself with yourself about what you're strong in and what you're weak in. And the better you perform, the more that voice says, *Hey, I'm kind of terrible at this.* It starts shrinking, and you need to make sure that you hear that all the time. That's part of fluid planning.

What I've had to understand is that you're building your ladder to heaven, but you must use whatever materials are around you to get there. It's whatever you have

around you. Life doesn't usually work in perfect sequential order.

These are the big goals. A lot of us have big goals. Therefore, we need to look at the things that we must do to reach them. How are you going to get to that point? You need to keep your eyes and ears and everything, all your awareness, open to the fact that it's not going to happen how you think it will.

So, you need to understand when the openings are there and when to take them. When the time comes that you need to pivot, you must pivot. But you can't get so rigid when it comes to planning that when things don't happen your way, you just slip out, go out of whack, and it takes you off your square that you need to stay in.

There are other important factors as well, such as mental health, mental toughness, mental stability, and seeing things in gray. There are a lot of different concepts that I try to introduce to students to help them through this process.

# DAVID CARTER

I had to reinvent myself and rediscover who I was after football because I played football my entire life. I'm very passionate about helping people, but it was hard for me to find my "why" and figure out how I was going to help people. How would I package myself in such a way where my value was easy to see and where I fit in and could thrive and grow?

I started by switching to a plant-based diet. I was helping myself because I had health issues while I was in the NFL, and eating a vegan diet helped that a lot. I was a 320-pound, very fit vegan playing nose tackle. It was at this time that I started my speaking journey.

I was helping people and sharing valuable information while sharing my journey. Next, I got into making documentaries, and that was also centered around helping people. I helped with both *The Game Changers* and *What the Health* documentaries. I also organized a concert series in New York.

Everything that I did was centered around helping people, and I stayed focused on my "why." Whenever I focused on my "why," I found energy from deep inside, a drive to find solutions.

I feel like I haven't worked a day in my life because everything that I've been doing has been helping people. Yes, I get paid for it, but it's extremely abundant because the real reward is that I help people and change lives. I give people useful information they didn't have before that could change the trajectory of their health situation or whatever their struggle is.

Figuring out my "why" was simple and natural because I've always been helpful and an empath and able to just feel the vibe of people. It's been easy for me to see what's going on, what the real issue is, and what the real solutions are. This is true for me in business, as well, and I use my understanding of the culture and people around me in my conversations and apply that to help make businesses more successful.

It's been that way since I was a little kid. My mom worked for the police department, and my dad was a computer tech. They had to have their clothes ironed and sharp. I would wake up in the morning and iron their clothes for them. I would also cook dinner for my family because they worked such long hours.

Helping others has always been something that's been ingrained in me. It's what I love to do. I just needed to figure out how to package that and put a motor behind it so I could drive in that lane.

I grew up in South Central Los Angeles in the hood. It was not the best neighborhood, to put it mildly. I lived right on the corner, too, which is the worst spot, and the street sign had bullet holes in it. Our house also had bullet holes, and my dad was actually at home when the house was shot at.

The first time I had a gun pointed at me, I was in the fourth grade. I was waiting at my bus stop at Crenshaw High School, and this guy pulled up. He was getting chased by the police, hopped out of his car, and pointed the gun at me as a hostage. They talked him down, and I ran into the school, crying.

My mom worked for the police department, and no one in our family was into gang life in any way. We played football because my parents said, "Get off the street. Go play football and spend all your time doing that." That saved us.

Being in that environment and seeing all the drugs and violence around me, I always thought, *What can I do to change this? What can I do to help?* It's painful to see friends you grew up with just start dropping off.

I grew up seeing gang culture, financial struggles, the day-to-day life struggles of the poor, mental and physical health issues, and the effects of a poor diet. I always paid you don't have the proper framework or support system, and you don't understand why you're even getting into it.

Students will say they're only there to play their sport, and they don't always realize they need a deeper understanding. They need to understand not only how the game is played but also how to be a part of a team.

To be an integral and important part of a team, you need to understand what you bring. What are your strengths? What are your weaknesses? Knowing your weaknesses is actually a strength, so you can work on that. You can also decide you will stick to your strengths and let other people excel where you're weak.

attention to that, to the state of the community, and I knew I needed to do something.

> **Stick to your strengths and let other people excel where you're weak.**

That's always been my mentality, even with my family. I was the biggest one of all the cousins; I was the defender. I had cousins who went to school with me, and they would get picked on because they were smaller. I was the one they looked at to protect them.

All these experiences helped shape me and my "why." They led me to the life I have today and all the amazing work I get to do.

Currently, the main business project I'm involved in is The Game Within the Game. It's a college-accredited program geared toward student-athletes. It's for everyone, not only student-athletes. When you're playing sports, it's a rough environment if

When you don't have that sense of clarity as an athlete, it can cause greater issues. It's the same issue that I was talking about in the hood. You see guys dropping off, mental health issues, getting into trouble with the law, and all kinds of stuff like that because it's a stressful environment, and it can cause a lot of issues and depression. So much of this negativity exists because they don't have the framework. If people have something to help guide them, it changes their experience and outcome.

The people who last the longest in sports are those who understand the mental side of the game, not just the physical side of the game. Sports are ninety percent mental and ten percent physical, especially at the professional level.

That's what we're working on with The Game Within the Game. And it's a college-accredited program through the Knowledge Innovation Center in Forbes Business School. It's in several universities right now across the country, and it's also available for high school students who can get dual credit for it if their school offers bridge programs. You can find more information at thegamewithinthegame.com.

Sometimes you don't know what next steps you should take, or your vision is a bit clouded. It helps to be your own mentor and be the one creating your objectives. Take a step back, evaluate yourself, and understand your strengths and your weaknesses. And when you understand yourself, that's when you understand how to improve yourself and utilize your resources. That is when you can transform your life.

Sometimes you forget, and sometimes you just can't see it because you're too close. You're in the thick of it. Before you can even ask someone else to help you out, you first have to understand that you need help and direction. You need to take a step back, reevaluate your situation, and make a simple pivot.

# CYNTHIA DAVIS

IMC stands for Incremental Monumental Change, and it's a philosophy and a way of leading. It's a way of being that recognizes how we can make mindful and purposeful decisions with cumulative purposeful actions every day that are in alignment with where we want to go. It includes our vision, our mission, and where we have an objective to take our business for growth.

IMC helps people recognize what is possible. It helps people ask questions like:

- How can I learn to make wiser decisions?

- How can I access, not only all the business instincts I've been taught, but a connection to a bigger possibility I can tune into within myself?
- How do I tap more deeply into my intuition, which helps me be more anticipatory about the future versus merely reactive?

Something happens in a business, and we can become very good at responding and reacting and maneuvering through all those challenges. Imagine being so connected to your future and what's possible and what you want to create that you can access a higher level of intuition that helps drive the wisest decisions.

Learning to do that and be that kind of leader is what I call Incremental Monumental Change. This philosophy states that the best way to predict the future is to create it.

Many of the amazing things we get to live with today would never exist if people didn't step into something new. Initially, there wasn't competition for things that now exist. They were new; they were innovative. That's why we have iPhones and so many other examples of business innovation.

If we only look at what is available in the current market and what our competition is doing, and what the current trends are, most of what we have access to today wouldn't exist. What I do involves tapping into that part of leadership and helping leaders access that. That creates transcendent leaders.

We hear about living in the top one percent, becoming part of the top one percent, and so on. Most people think that it's referring only to monetary success. I have redefined that because it's not just about monetary success, but it is also about how to create success and value in your life where you can now empower and give back. That's the thinking of a transcendent leader.

A transcendent leader is someone who has a consciousness of that. There's the achievement of success, but fulfillment comes when you're able to share that on a greater scale. There's an impact you can make in the world in terms of uplifting all of humanity. When you do that, you've transcended the

business model of acquiring and doing more. Transcendent leadership involves thinking, *I want to do more, but I also want to do so much better, to be so much better.*

Transcendent leaders have a vision that is bigger than themselves, and they must engage other people to be part of it. Those are the kind of leaders I love to work with. Those are the kind of leaders with whom I have the privilege of working. The

much better than growing a business on the other side.

A big part of the incremental monumental change process is helping people dispel and suspend some of their disbeliefs. Get clear on what it is that you envision and what you want to create, and hold that with such clarity that you embody it in who you are and become the leader of that before you've actually realized it.

> **" Transcendent leaders have a vision that is bigger than themselves, and they must engage other people to be part of it. "**

key for me and my mission is to ask, "How can I work with conscious leaders, transcendent leaders, and visionary leaders and support them in such a way that they can make a powerful impact without burnout, without the constant anxiety or stress?"

Is there another way of connecting to your vision where you can have more confidence, more certainty, more alignment with your true north, and master who you are and how you show up so you don't end up with burnout? How can you live so you don't have the anxiety and the stress that I once did? I've lived on both sides of that equation, and growing a business from this side of the equation is so

Often, we get so caught up in business, and when I'm working with leaders, they say, "Oh yeah, yeah, yeah. I know that. I've heard that." And yet, they haven't done the work of really understanding that for themselves and their business. You accomplish a lot simply by starting right there with that process and gaining clarity. Ask yourself, *What's the problem that I'm solving? Who is it for?*

The next thing that we go through is what I call the obvious choice solution. How do you get to be? What is it that you have to be to become the obvious choice in the marketplace? If I'm the obvious choice in the marketplace, I'm not that concerned about what the competitors are doing.

Part of my job as a business leader is to understand that and to stay aware, but I'm not trying to be a little better than them. I'm chasing my vision. I'm working toward maximizing the value that I bring to what I do. The client can see it and say, "I want that because you've become the obvious choice."

I mostly work with technology companies and technology-service-oriented companies, and I help them create the ability to not just sit there and compare themselves to the competition but to articulate how it is that they're hands down the most valuable choice in the marketplace, the *obvious* choice in the marketplace. That's such a better place to be, and we show them how to become that obvious choice.

We also teach all the business processes that go with that in terms of how to run your business and measure it. We deal a lot with how to maximize the value of your business and think about your exit strategy long before you get to that point. We have a lot of really good, basic business tools we support them with that give them clear visibility into their business. And so much of it is the mindset with which they approach and view their business.

We help them to see the unseen because it's very difficult to see it for yourself. I had a client the other day who said, "Okay, I guess I have to do this marketing thing, this necessary evil of selling."

And I said, "That's what you're going to call them? The necessary evil? You should be in love with what it is you do for your clients because you know what value you add to their lives. If you see helping your clients as a necessary evil, I think we might have a problem."

He wasn't even aware he had said it. As soon as I brought it to his awareness, he said, "Oh my God, you're absolutely right."

I think that there are probably many leaders who feel that it's acceptable to be an okay leader, and for them, they can do their thing. But there are those who have a dream for tomorrow that's bigger than where they are today, an inner drive that says there's more, and sticking with the status quo is not sufficient. That's who we love to work with. That's who we want to work with.

I abhor mediocrity. I abhor the status quo. Sometimes, somebody will call me and ask about what we do, and I'll ask them to tell me what they want to achieve. If they tell me they want to improve their business by ten percent, I tell them we're probably not for them because anybody could get them a ten-percent improvement.

You can go anywhere. You can even read a book, do one or two things, and achieve a ten-percent improvement if you're smart. But if you really want to make an impact that's much bigger than yourself, that you can't do yourself, you must enroll others in your mission. For us, the clients we work with have that passion and drive, but they need guidance to help them learn how to shift their thought process to what they want to create versus what they want to avoid happening.

businesses. Their business is an extension of who they are, and it's incredible.

My path here wasn't a straight shot, of course, and I think a lot of people have the same experience. We learn these lessons, and then, somehow, they formulate where we end up in life. That was true for me. I was very entrepreneurial from a young age. I watched my grandmother, who was an amazing entrepreneur, build a business at a time when that was unheard of. I knew

> **If you really want to make an impact that's much bigger than yourself, that you can't do yourself, you must enroll others in your mission.**

That's the sweet spot, and that's where I see amazing entrepreneurs and leaders making an impact on humanity through their businesses. It is incredibly powerful for me to work with these business leaders so they can make an impact through their

that in me was a sense of freedom and the ability to change people's lives and do big things. I've always wanted that, but I was raised with the safety net of *getting an education, getting a job, going to school, getting a job, staying there for thirty years, and retiring.* I wanted to please my parents.

I have six siblings, so there was not a lot to go around, plus I was a middle child. I had two older sisters, and I can never remember a time in my childhood when I had a new dress. Everything we had were hand-me-downs. I remember thinking, *I'm going to do anything and everything not to live life this way.* I hated hearing that we couldn't afford that, I couldn't do this, or that we couldn't go on vacation.

I did all that was expected of me, and I excelled. I pushed myself and drove myself to academics and the military, and then I got a good job. As an athlete, I was always at the head of the pack in everything. I always excelled. I worked in the corporate world, and even then, I did things unheard of for a woman as I advanced in my career.

But I wasn't a corporate person. I had to color between the lines, and I didn't like that. I did really well. And I stayed with it for many, many years, and I learned so much. I had a phenomenal career, but I knew that I had to be in a job that had a lot of autonomy where I was running a business within a business, or I wasn't happy. I wasn't good at not being an entrepreneur. So, I found ways to bring my entrepreneurial spirit into my life.

I remember having a job where I had to drive an hour and a half, one way, back and forth. And I turned my car into a learning center. I listened to so many amazing people. Back then, Tony Robbins had his *Get The Edge* program, and I'd listen to Brian Tracy, Earl Nightingale, Og Mandino, and Bob Proctor. Bob wrote the foreword to my book years later. Go figure.

I listened to all these amazing people, and it didn't only shape my thinking, it also shaped my actions. I set goals, and I was very good at it. But I learned I was doing all of that to avoid something—to avoid lack, to avoid not having enough, to avoid my children hearing, "We can't afford that." I was driven by wanting to avoid some of the experiences that actually shaped me as a young child. I would get to a certain level of money prestige, and then I'd self-sabotage, and I'd lose it.

One day I was listening to Wayne Dyer, and I realized that everything I was doing was in that direction, wanting to avoid something. I was instinctively an amazing decision maker and an amazing manager, but I wasn't connected to a future vision and building what I was passionate about. Even though I had a vision and I had goals, I didn't have passion because I was in a suit in the wrong place. I told myself that when I left the corporate world, I would start my own business as a consulting firm that would do for those business leaders what I always wish someone had done for me.

That's when I started the consulting firm Radiant Blue, and that's exactly what we do. We have an amazing consulting firm. We are the consultants I wish I had when I was running a $2 billion business. I wish I had been given the advice I now give our clients. When I left, everybody thought I was crazy because I was at the pinnacle of my career.

It was also the first time I felt scared. I didn't even know how to use Excel. I had a staff to do all these things for me. I was fearful, and I didn't want anyone to know.

Despite those fears, I felt at home. I felt more freedom than I had with all my previous work combined. I finally followed my passion for working with business leaders and entrepreneurs and doing what I'm doing now. I feel like I'm building into the future from a place of passion. I'm building something important, and it's incredibly fulfilling. All the success markers I thought of in the past keep coming but in a different way.

Now, I get to work with our clients, not only to help them see what they can't see for themselves but also to get their heads and hearts wrapped around their business. When that happens, it's a whole new ball game. You get to live day by day, moment to moment. You start asking, "Is this in alignment with where I'm going?"

When you stay in tune with that level of elevation of your vision and where you are, you see opportunities that you wouldn't have seen. You start to experience and meet people in new situations. You experience and see what is in alignment with where you're going. When you stay in alignment with that, you get to see and experience life in a whole new way.

# *MITCH RUSSO*

My involvement in the business coaching community spans decades. I have helped other companies by being a coach, and over the years, I have perfected a process that allows companies to expand very rapidly because we are not typically focusing on the things they're used to focusing on.

When I work with a client, we talk about business strategy. Strategy is a combination of tactics and philosophy. The behind the way a person operates is really what their business is. Let's break that down a little further.

If you don't know your own "why," then it's going to be very hard to understand why you do the things you do. For example, my "why" is to find a better way. What that means is that when I look at anything, I immediately start to uncover better ways to do what it is I'm looking at or seeing or involved in.

When people ask me to join some form of a collaboration group, for example, I'm the guy with the ideas because I see things from a different perspective. I do not look to invent anything new unless it's important to move forward in that way. I look to find a better way. That's my "why."

In my business life, it's been incredibly useful. It's really why I've started all of my businesses. I run into a problem that I can't solve, or I look for something to help me, and I can't find it. I have to invent it. That's really what my entrepreneurial journey has been about—finding a better way.

I feel like it's easier for me because earlier in my life I was able to uncover my true purpose. However, your true purpose alone is

that doesn't fit your "why," then it's going to be like sandpaper on glass. It won't move smoothly at all.

I take my clients through a system I've worked with over many years. In about a half hour, we uncover people's true purpose. Once we do that and we know their "why,"

> **If I help a hundred coaches who each have a hundred clients, I'm helping a lot of people in a short period.**

not as valuable until you couple it with your "why" and then use it to drive your mission, your true mission.

Everybody's true purpose is the same—to help others. But how you help others is dramatically different from person to person. If you go about helping others in a way

then we look at their business and we say, "You know what? This is not what you told me your true purpose is.

We then have a few choices. Should we scrap this business and start over, focusing entirely on your true purpose and your true mission? Or can we view this business

from a different perspective? Can we adjust the way we see this business, and more importantly, the way we operate this business to fit the true purpose and true mission?

That's where I come in because that's what I'm able to do very quickly.

Once we do that, then the next step is to create what I would call the business operating environment for my clients. I build a mind map of their entire organization, and I'm usually able to do that in about two hours. In two hours, we have every single element of their business, every single element of what we are planning going forward, and now we can break that down with a timeline.

Step one, find a true purpose. Step two, map the business and assign priorities. Step three, build a timeline. And then work together, week after week, to accomplish those goals so that at the end of our engagement, you have vastly changed how you see your business: You have increased the productivity of yourself and your team, you have increased revenue, you may have added new products or new ways to market those same products, and you're a happier person.

I have encapsulated a lot into my book, *Coach Elevation*. The whole point of *Coach Elevation* is to teach the method I've just described. Typically, I address coaches. The reason I serve coaches is that one of my true missions is to change the world. I'm just one person; I can't change the world.

What I *can* do is to help those world changers be better at what they do. Coaches are world changers. They change the world one person at a time. If I could help a hundred coaches who each have a hundred clients, I'm helping a lot of people in a matter of a short period—maybe a year or less.

I believe that this process is fundamental to trying to accomplish anything. You can also use this true purpose process that I blueprint in my book *Coach Elevation* in your personal relationships.

Imagine your spouse comes to you and says, "Honey, I just want to share something with you. I want to talk to you." And then they start telling you what they perceive as a problem, maybe in their work life, maybe at home, or wherever.

What you might say, as a find-a-better-way person, is, "Well, if you did this, you could fix that. And by the way, you might want to try that." I think you probably know how well that works. Not very well at all because all they really wanted was to be heard. (It

took a couple of marriages for me to figure this out.)

By understanding your "why" and your true purpose and then operating together as a couple, you can change everything. That's why I believe it's so important.

When I look back at my own life, I see that I've accomplished a lot. I've built companies, I've worked with Tony Robbins as a partner (we had a company exceeding $25 million in revenue), I've built software companies, and right now, I have another software company focused on the work I do with coaches called ClientFol.io. These companies are all designed to do the same thing.

Everything I've ever done was about coaching and training, about helping people accelerate and expand their abilities. That's what I believe a great coach is supposed to do.

In the early days, when I started Timeslips Corporation in 1985, I built that company around a problem I was trying to solve. That pivoted into a completely different product, but a much more viable and successful product than the first idea. I never would've found that idea if I wouldn't have stayed on course on purpose to find a better way, which, again, is my "why."

I think the most important thing about anything you do is to be fully engaged—mind, body, and spirit. I know that's a very general term, but what I mean by that is, if you have the wrong focus when you enter a business or a personal relationship, it's going to be much harder for that relationship to succeed. It can succeed, but it will be much harder.

If you're focused on money when you start a business, it could succeed, but it's going to be much harder. In addition, if you're focused on personal growth, as I think most people figure out after they've started a business, you'll succeed in a more fulfilling way. Push yourself past your comfort zone because everything you are afraid of is exactly where you need to go.

Business is about testing all of our abilities every day. As we grow as business owners, as we accelerate this process of expanding our business, we accelerate our own personal growth.

As business owners, we bring other families along with us—the people we employ. You can't just be the guy who writes the check. You are the person who leads these people.

Help the people who surround you to expand their abilities. Help them push past their boundaries. They will appreciate it and will stay with you and be loyal. Those are exactly the type of organizations I like to build.

# MICHAEL MARKIEWICZ

I used to only describe myself as a CPA with a CPA practice, but I have expanded into so many other ventures that I prefer not to pigeonhole myself that way. I'm a CPA by day, providing high-level services to high-net-worth individuals, small businesses, entertainment professionals, fashion industry professionals, and many others.

But I've also become involved in a number of other endeavors. I recently wrote a chapter for a book about entrepreneurship for leaders that will be published soon. In my chapter, I wrote about tax planning for high-net-worth individuals, and I go into detail about a number of significant tax planning opportunities. I guess I can now call myself a soon-to-be-published author.

I have also become involved in a film development project where I'm an executive producer. I've read the first two-thirds of the script, and I'm waiting for the final third to read. Being a very visual person, as I read through the first two-thirds of it, I had a movie going on in my head about what this was going to look like. Whether that actually pans out to be what my movie is, I don't know, but it's fun to imagine. I'm likely going to have a very small role in the film, which is also quite exciting.

Over the years, I've I have provided a lot of services in the entertainment space as a CPA, where I provide business management services for actors, directors, producers, and writers.

Business management services entails handling all aspects of their financial affairs. We understand their contracts and how much they're supposed to be paid. We pay their bills for them. We do their tax planning and tax compliance. It runs the gamut of pretty much everything and anything having to do with their financial lives.

From there, my practice evolved into providing production accounting services for films. As a film is being made, I get engaged to do all the production accounting. It's a specialized kind of work because most states and some cities provide some kind of film tax credit if you film in their jurisdiction. It brings a lot of money into that state or city. There's a definitive way that we have to do the accounting for that purpose.

I've also become, over the years, an investor in live performances. I've invested in a few Broadway shows, a number of touring companies, and other live shows in Las Vegas, some in the UK, and some in Australia.

In addition to that, I'm the CFO of a private-equity firm.

Our private-equity firm's largest project currently is in the mining space. We own precious metal mines in Colorado, and we mine gold, silver, platinum, and some industrial metals as well. I was able to tour the mines recently, and it was pretty amazing to see what we have accomplished in the six years that we have been at it.

How did I get into this? I have to go back to how I got into becoming a CPA. When I was in undergraduate school, I was in a liberal arts program. They didn't have a business or accounting program, and I was a double major in economics and sociology. In the economics department, there was a basic accounting course, which I took. I aced it with my hands tied behind my back; it just came so naturally to me.

I went on to graduate school almost immediately and entered a Master of Science in Accounting program. Through that program, I was immediately placed with one of the big international accounting firms in Boston, which is where I'm originally from. And the rest is history.

At one point in my career, I went to work for a business management firm based in New York. The client roster was the crème de la crème of people in the entertainment industry, and I got to work with several of these people over the years. It was a whole new area for me, but I loved it, and the business management services I provide grew out of that experience.

Getting into the production accounting side of things happened because a particular lawyer in the entertainment space here in New York called me one day and said, "Hey, Michael, I've got this new client. They're out of Spain, but they're filming in the US, and I'd like you to meet them."

I met them, but I had no idea how to do production accounting at that point. But, as paraphrased from Richard Branson, when someone asks you to do something, even if you don't know how to do it, say yes and then figure it out. That's exactly what I did.

In terms of investing in live theatre and other live productions, I know a number of people here in New York who are theatre producers. Over time, they started asking me if I would be interested in participating as an investor in a particular production. I jumped in with both feet, and in the process, I got burned a few times, but learned very quickly what to look for in a production from the financial point of view. Other than the glamorous part of meeting some celebrities, I came to realize that, while that is exciting, I'd rather make money at it.

I'm currently an executive producer on one film that is currently in development.

An executive producer does two things, one of which is to provide money for the project. I'm not the only executive producer on these. If you've ever watched credits on a film or TV show, there are any number of executive producers on any one production. They all provide some money, as do the producers. This is to fund the development and the actual filming.

The second thing an executive producer does is to read the script as it is being written. Another potential aspect—and in this case, it looks like it'll happen—is I will get a small role in the film. I'll then be able to add that to my CV and say I'm an actor, too.

In the business management space, I was once assigned the account of one of the most prolific Hollywood producers ever, so I worked very closely with him. When I say prolific, this guy produced films and theater. He's a name you would recognize, and I'm sure you'd recognize the films. In addition to doing all the other things that producers and executive producers do, he actually got involved on the set of the production.

He'd work very closely with the director. And because he had such a forceful personality, if he didn't like something that the director did, he'd make him or her change it. The guy was brilliant. Many of his film projects came from books that he'd read. If he liked a book, he'd option it for a film, which meant that he then had the rights to make a film of it.

He had a reputation for being very mean, tough, and abusive. When I first started working with him, every single morning, before I even got into my office, there'd be a voicemail from his office. Not from him, but from one of his production assistants, saying, "Hey, I've got so-and-so on the phone for you; please return the call."

These messages would show up around 7:00 in the morning, and I'd get into my office by 8:00 or 8:30. Initially, I thought, *This guy is calling me? Wow, that's amazing.* I would immediately call back, but, of course, he was never available to take my call.

After several months, I came to realize that he didn't actually call to have a conversation with me. He just wanted to know that I was there and that I was working for him.

I also saw how abusive he could be to some of the people that worked directly for him. I didn't work directly for him, however. I was part of the business management firm, and we provided services to him.

I worked for him all this time, and we would pay his bills after he approved them. His little squiggly signature was well known to me. In those days, we'd prepare all the checks, send them by messenger to his office, then he would sign them, send them back, and we'd mail them out.

One day, we received some expense reports that he had approved from his production assistants. He called me up and started

screaming. He said, "How in the world can you approve this and write a check for this? Don't you see this guy is padding his expense report? You should know better." And on and on he went. When he finally stopped to take a breath, I said to him, "Yes, but you approved it." He said, "That doesn't matter. I don't care." And he hung up the phone on me.

The next day, I spoke to him, and it was like nothing had ever happened. So, I wear it as a badge of honor to say, "Okay, I've been on the receiving end of that, and I survived, and I'm fine."

One thing I always say to myself, having worked and continuing to work in the entertainment space, is that I love the fact

> **Don't get all starry-eyed about celebrities. Most of them are just regular people like you and me.**

As soon as he hung up the phone, I felt the blood drain from my head down into my feet. I must have been ghost white. I sat at my desk for a while, and I thought about it. Slowly but surely, the blood rose back to my head. I realized that this wasn't about me. This was about him.

He was having a moment, or a day, or a morning, and he had to take it out on somebody. And I happened to be a convenient target.

that I'm on the periphery of it—on the outside looking in, in a sense. That is because the film and television world, in particular, perhaps the theater world as well, can be a vicious, brutal world.

I'm fortunate that I can be involved in the entertainment space but not have to deal with that side of it. I'm not an actor or a director or a producer. I'm on the periphery, working with those people but looking in from the outside.

I think anybody who wants to get involved in the entertainment industry should know two things. One, don't get all starry eyed about celebrities. I found, and I think a lot of people have found, that the majority of them are just regular people like you and me. They get up in the morning, and they put their pants on one leg at a time, just like we do.

In our society, we put them on a pedestal. We watch *Entertainment Tonight*, and we read entertainment magazines and blogs

online. I caution people to be careful about being starry-eyed about celebrities. This is their work, their job.

I attend a lot of theater here in New York, and frequently, in addition to the people on stage, there are celebrities in the audience. They want to see the show the same as we do. I've often seen them, and I'd be sitting there next to my husband, and I'd say, "Oh look, there's so and so." And it's like, "Okay, now let's watch the show."

The other thing that I think people should know is if you're looking to get into working in this industry, make sure you establish a boundary between being in it and being on the periphery of it. When you're on the periphery, there are some great perks, like getting invited to opening nights or a film premiere and the after-party.

You get to mingle with a lot of celebrities, as it were, but stay within your boundaries. Stay in your lane. I remember one time, years ago, I went to the Grammy Awards in LA, and then I went to an after-party. People started asking, "Who are you, and what do you do?" I said, "Well, I'm just here attending."

The attitude that most of those people had was, *He can't do anything for me, so I'm going to go on to the next person.*

I was with a friend of mine, and I said, "Let's play a little game. When the next person comes up and asks us that question, we're going to say, 'We're publicists from New York. We're looking for the next great act.'" Suddenly, everybody was all over us. I would then say to these people, "Sorry, can't talk. We've got to go on to the next party." You can have fun with it without actually jumping into it with both feet.

# HERB "FLIGHT TIME" LANG

I grew up in a small town in Arkansas. My mother had me when she was seventeen, and by the time she was twenty-five, she had six of us. I was fortunate enough to have a lot of aunts and uncles, and grandparents that were around to help mold me. I spent a lot of time with my grandparents at a young age, and I received a lot of wisdom from them.

My grandparents were about giving and inspiring and creating hope and trying to make things better for people in the community. They would go around and check on people. My grandmother would walk to older people's houses and check to see how they were doing.

We would go to churches and revivals all around the South. I remember looking at people and the way that the preachers were preaching. People were looking for hope. Even my grandmother lived off of prayer and hope. Being raised around that showed me the power of kindness, and kindness is what led me to where I am right now.

Kindness is responsible for me receiving a basketball scholarship to Centenary College in Shreveport, Louisiana. It was because someone spoke up for me. The school had never seen me play, but I was class president, had good ACT scores, and I was an Allstate player in Arkansas. They offered me a scholarship without even seeing me

# KINDNESS

play. In fact, they never even brought me on a recruiting visit.

And that's just one of the first examples of kindness leading up to my opportunity with the Globetrotters, which came from a friendship I made at college. A friend of mine who played soccer in my college went to a Globetrotter game. At the time, I had graduated and was working as a personal trainer, making seven dollars an hour. We were roommates, and he came back from the game with a program with an 800 number on it and said, "I just went to the Globetrotters game, and you can do the stuff that they're doing."

I thought, *Man, I'm not trying to play for the Globetrotters; I'm trying to go to the NBA.* During that time, the NBA had a lockout, so I wasn't able to go to their Portsmouth mini-camps or their Chicago summer league camps. I ended up going back to school and finishing my degree, which was one of the best things I ever did.

During that process of working, I realized how much I really did want to play the game of basketball. And then, a couple of weeks after my roommate brought that program home, I said, "Hey, man, where's that program at? I think I still have something to offer the game of basketball." I sent them a video of some of my basketball highlights in college, as well as me winning the dunk contest the year before. And they put me down for their training camp!

Over my career, I traveled to many countries around the world with the Globetrotters, plus I visited every state, met President Obama twice, met Pope Francis, and met many other wonderful people along the way.

One day, it dawned on me that everything that happened in my life was through kindness. People didn't have to step up for me or say things; they believed in me. They saw something in me. That's what I want to give to people. I want to give people hope. You lost your job; I lost my job, too. It's okay. This is what you get to keep doing. You had other dreams when you were younger.

My wife and I have been married since February 22, 2022, and I have a son who's sixteen and a daughter who's fifteen. After my career ended, I wanted to continue being an example for them. I didn't want them to have to listen to, "Oh, well, your dad, back in the day, he used to be...."

While one of my goals was to become a professional athlete, I also dreamed of performing. Michael Jackson was one of my heroes, and I loved how he could dance. I wanted to be creative like that. Everything I was able to see during my Globetrotter years, such as being in commercials, being in

deal on. It's going a different way, but I still get opportunities like that.

It's about not giving up and realizing that if you treat people well, they will want to be around you. If I had been a jerk during my time on *The Amazing Race* or my time during the Globetrotters, there's no way that this well-respected, Emmy-winning creator would have allowed me to come into his office with his management team and talk about what I have and actually believe in it.

My kindness movement is now a way of life. It's easy for me because I've been conditioned for it all my life, whereas some people find it hard to wake up in the morning and be nice to people. That's my motivation. I

> **It's about being kind, not only to other people but also to yourself.**

movies, being able to speak in schools and at Fortune 500 companies—I accumulated all these experiences and used them to push myself even further. This includes creating my own brand swag ball during COVID and writing my own book when I retired from the Globetrotters. I had the opportunity to co-write a book, *Cracking the Rich Code*, with Jim Britt and Kevin Harrington. I will continue living my life as an example for others, especially young people.

Everything good in my life came through kindness and relationships I built along the way. Even with sports game show ideas. From my experiences on *The Amazing Race*, I was able to go into Bertram van Munster's office and pitch two or three television show ideas, one of which we actually had a

get excited to wake up and send positivity out to all the people who follow me on social media, all the people who are within my immediate family, and my outside circle—seventy-five to one hundred people a day. I get to get up at 5:00, seven days a week, and tell people, "Hey, you can do it. Keep going." I get to post videos of me at forty-six years old, still dunking a basketball and getting shots up for two hours after walking two miles and after working out on my toning machine.

It's about being kind, not only to other people but also to yourself. I get to do these things, and I get it all in return. When I'm sending seventy-five to one hundred messages to different people in the morning, I'm getting thirty-five to forty back messages back.

"Thank you. I appreciate it. You inspired me today." And that fills me up. I know that people are paying attention when I get messages like, "Man, I rode my bike twelve miles today after seeing you work out," or "I started eating differently this week because of something that you said." That's what it's all about. It's a movement, and it's catching on.

It didn't get all the momentum I hoped to get at the beginning, but everything happens when it's supposed to. Even having the opportunity to be part of the Bellwether Alliance and having an opportunity to be a part of this magazine article is an example that I'm moving in the right direction because these opportunities haven't been presented to me before. These are the next chapters in my book. I'm living my movie right now.

When I talk to groups of students, I always talk about kindness. I also talk about a program I have called KEYS—Keeping Excitement for Your Success. I also bring kids up to do Globetrotters tricks and give them pop sockets that say, "Keeping Excitement for Your Success" or "Kindness is Free." I have lanyards that I put around their neck for coming up, and, when they come up, not only do they learn a trick, but I also ask them what that word means to them, and they give an example for the audience. They learn it's about never giving up on your dreams and being kind along the way.

I also have about five games I bring into the schools. Typically, it's a mini basketball hoop, a soccer net, a football, a baseball, and even golf. We'll do three or five sports while at an elementary school. I'll team a kindergartner

up with a fifth grader, a second grader with a fourth grader, just showing you how you get to work together, no matter the difference in age.

It's about putting people together and making connections at a young age, something I learned while traveling around the world. And the same thing with the older kids. If I speak to a freshman class, I'll ask myself, *What do I get to share with these young people? What was I doing in ninth grade? What would I want to hear from me if I was speaking to myself in ninth grade?* That's what I'll share with these kids. I'll tell them stories. I'll share what my high school coach shared with me as a freshman and what was ahead. It all comes together.

If I'm speaking at a business event or an event for people who've lost their jobs, I might talk about how I got the phone call from the Globetrotters after eighteen years, plus three times on *The Amazing Race.* I went from spinning the basketball on Pope Francis's finger in 2015 to spinning the wheels on my car for Lyft, driving around picking up people to eventually going door-to-door selling insurance. It's about never giving up and realizing that if you did it once, you can do it again. I love inspiring people through my stories and being an example through my actions and what I create along the way, whether it's creating documentaries or sports game shows.

My dream is to own a professional sports franchise, and my ultimate vision with that is to spread kindness throughout the world through the world's team. I think it's important to be kind just to be kind and not because of what you might gain from it. When you work that way, you'll see magic happening around you that you couldn't even imagine. Make it a habit to be kind to yourself every day. For me, that starts with new habits.

After I left the Globetrotters, I started meditating. That helps me to create the days I want. I also started walking every day. That puts me in touch with nature and allows me to think about how this world was created. It grounds me.

Be kind to yourself first. Take time for yourself and realize that you get one chance at this life. Everyone you watch on social media or on the movie screens, including me, has been through a lot of the same things that you're going through. They're human. They have parents, grandparents, or children, just like you. If they can do it, then you can do it. Just put your mind to it and start conditioning yourself mentally and emotionally. And one person at a time, you get to change the world.

# CHASE BARFIELD

One of my first business ventures was as a partner in a construction company. Even though I was a partner, I also ran heavy machinery. I had to do the excavation and got tired of the weather controlling whether we worked or not. Around this time, my wife came to me and said, "You can't work with your back forever." So, I decided to go into the IT world and founded an IT company.

I was quite successful at growing the company and getting it in the black relatively quickly. I was noticed by other people who asked me to be partners with them, be on their board, and try to help replicate my success in their companies. I was in my early to mid-twenties at this time. Most of what

I accomplished was through sheer will and determination, not necessarily because I had tons of experience or education.

At some point, I was actively involved in over a dozen businesses, which I wouldn't recommend to anyone. It really took a big hit to my ego because I was someone who could move the needle considerably, and I wasn't moving any needles. I felt like one of those guys you see on TV where they're spinning several plates. I was running back and forth, spinning all these plates so that they wouldn't fall, but I was not getting anything done.

My wife's a very wise person. She told me that I suffered from the-grass-is-greener syndrome. She said, "The grass would be pretty damn green if you just watered where you stood." I was involved in too many things, so I agreed, and I sold off or merged multiple different businesses that I was involved in. I quit a few boards and narrowed everything down.

I realized that I loved getting things started. It was exciting to be involved. Whenever I wondered about a new industry, I didn't think to read about it or ask someone about it. Instead, I would start a business and learn trial by fire. I do not recommend this approach.

I founded Take Control with the intent of helping C-level and principal-level executives to take their personal objectives and align them with their professional objectives so they have one plan rather than two separate plans. Small things like, if you had a personal plan that you wanted to visit an island in Greece, and if you have a legitimate business reason to go there, then we can combine your personal plan with your legitimate business plan and tick off two boxes at the same time.

Also, it scratched the itch I had to use my creative brain. I love creating plans. A lot of people would find what I do to be boring, but I love to create plans, identify the resources needed, acquire those resources, and help to execute the plan. I like to do it in different industries. By working with different people in different industries, I scratched that itch, so I didn't have to start or get involved in all these other companies myself. I did it as an extension of the services I offered inside Take Control. That's how my background led me to Take Control's first iteration.

I started working with these clients on an annual contract to help them take their personal objectives and their professional objectives and create one main plan. Sometimes it would take longer than a year, but it was one-year minimum because these people had been doing the wrong things for a long time.

After a while, I noticed that many of these business leaders looked at me more like a security blanket, for lack of a better term. I wasn't helping to achieve objectives anymore. They were just asking my advice and opinion on their own decisions, which they were fully capable of making on their own.

I didn't feel like I was delivering full value to them, so like a mama bird kicking her babies out of the nest when she feels they can fly, I started firing clients. I would tell them, "I don't think that we should renew. If you still need my help, my phone's always open, and you can call me later. I can give you a little guidance, but I don't think that you need me as a strategic advisor moving forward."

They felt they were receiving full value, but I wasn't delivering value in a way that got me excited. I didn't feel fulfilled doing that. I felt fulfilled up to the point where I felt they should be able to make these decisions on their own, and they were fully capable of doing so. They went on to be successful after I told them that I didn't think we should work together anymore.

So, my model migrated into a project-based contract. We had a start time and a finish time with one specific objective to achieve. At the end of that, if they wanted to renew on some other objective, and I was agreeable, then we would.

I like the variety and the challenge of creating these strategies. I learned that my superpower is to see things that others don't. I have a business partner who says he likes me to be involved because I see what he calls potholes. I see down the road, and I know how to plan to avoid them, fill them in, take a different route, or do whatever else is necessary.

I make a much greater impact whenever I'm not reading emails or answering phone calls. I have three sons, and two of them work with me. They are training at different levels on how to take over project management for these different clients. That is what I call $10 or even $100 an hour stuff that I do not get involved in. I'm much better whenever I'm involved in $1,000 or even sometimes $10,000 an hour stuff. That actually helps me to help more people. I get to work in my genius zone.

> **Go after your actual "why" because most people die with the regret of not being true to themselves.**

I'm good at developing strategic plans. I enjoy being industry and geographically agnostic and able to create plans because I know what is fundamental to their success, depending upon what their objectives are. I no longer operate from sheer will and determination. I have a lot of experience and education under my belt.

I won't grow Take Control beyond a certain number of clientele because I'm at a place in my life where I don't have to take on more active hours of work. In helping to lead clients through what they've done, other opportunities have opened up that have allowed me and my partners to acquire equitable positions, passive income opportunities, and more, along the way. I talk to people from all over the world in many situations and scenarios. Sometimes, instead of them paying for my service with cash, they pay with equity or service for something else that's a value exchange.

My definition of retirement is not needing to work. It's not reaching the age of 65 or anything like that. My purpose on this planet is to build a generational wealth machine and teach my sons how to manage and grow it. I will probably do something in this capacity until I no longer draw breath on this planet. I don't see a time where I'm not going to be either doing it myself or helping my sons tweak the engine, so to speak, to keep this machine running perpetually.

It took me a while to realize what my "why" was. For someone to understand what motivates and drives them, I would challenge them to take the time to sit with themselves and try to realize what their "why" is. Sometimes it's super big and scares them, but my advice is to live to be your true self. Go after your actual "why" because most people die with the regret of not being true to themselves. I am unashamedly true to myself about what I want to accomplish. That is very powerful.

# ADVERTISERS

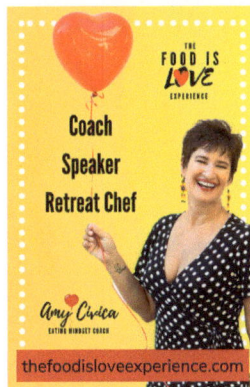

www.ingramcontent.com/pod-product-compliance
Lightning Source LLC
Chambersburg PA
CBHW041453210326
41599CB00004B/232